HIPPOS

Let's Meet Mr. Hippo

The hippopotamus or hippo, is a large,
mostly herbivorous mammal
in sub-Saharan Africa.

"Hippopotamus" comes from two Greek words, Hippo meaning horse and potamos meaning river. That is why it is also known as, "River Horse".

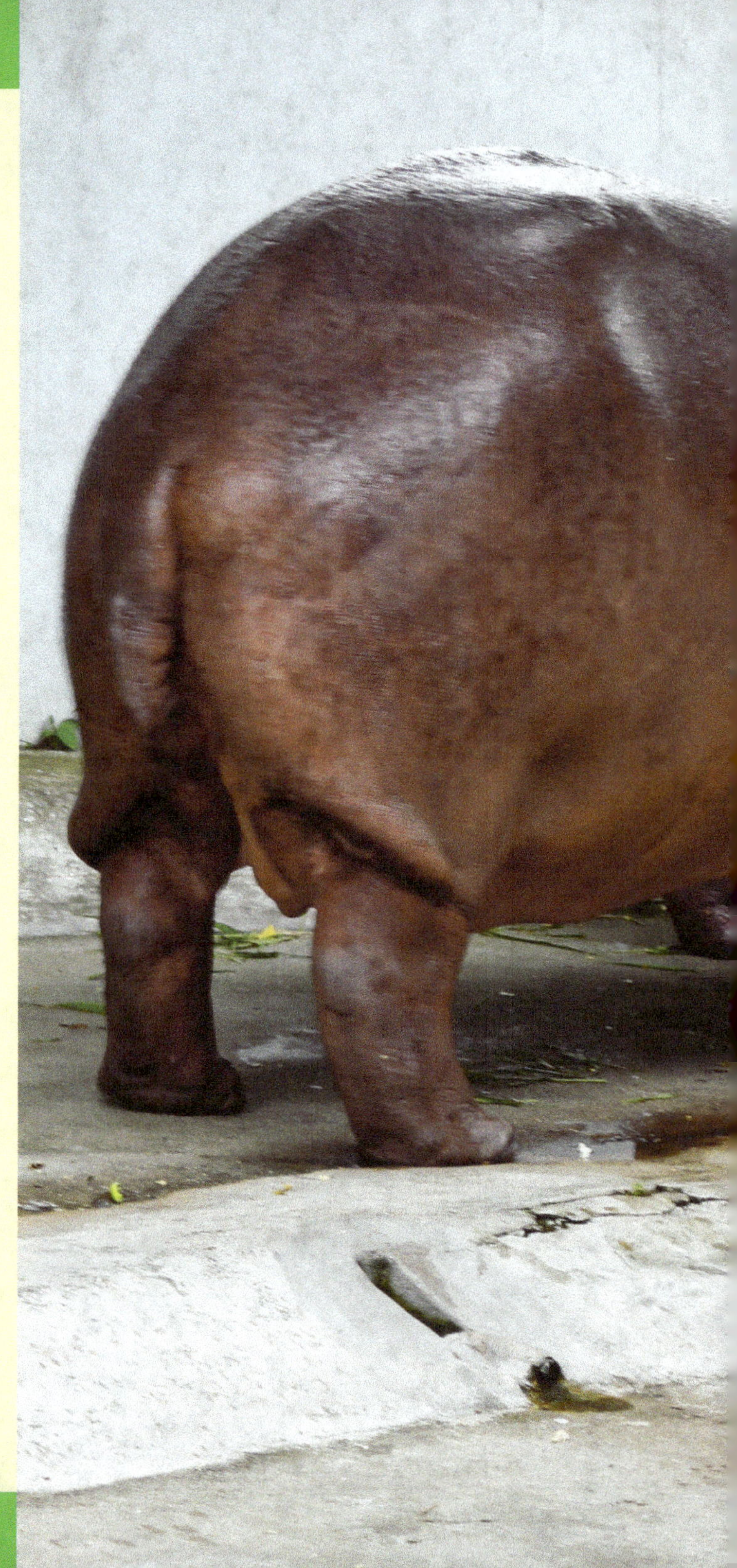

The hippopotamus is generally considered the third largest land mammal, after the White rhinoceros and elephant.

Hippopotamuses spend a large amount of time in water such as rivers, lakes and swamps.

An adult
Hippo needs
to resurface
every 3 – 5mins
to breathe.
The process
of surfacing
and breathing
is automatic,
and even a
hippo sleeping
underwater will
rise and breathe
without waking.

Hippopotamus live in groups and there are usually 10 to 30 hippos in a herd.

Resting in water helps keep hippopotamuses temperature down.

A male hippopotamus is called a 'bull' and a female hippopotamus is called a 'cow'.

Hippo calves weigh approximately 45kg at birth. Each female has only one calf every two years.

Hippos will travel on land for up to 10km to feed. They spend four to five hours grazing and can consume 68 kg of grass each night.

Hippos yawn, it is a threatening sign by them. The texture of the teeth is similar to the tusks of the elephants, that means they are also made up of ivory and they can grow up to 1 foot.

One thing that differentiates the Hippo's milk with others' is its color. Hippos are the only mammals that produce pink milk.

The
hippopotamus
is one of the
most aggressive
creatures in the
world and is
often regarded
as one of the
most dangerous
animals in Africa.

Hippos can be very territorial and will fight with other hippos over territory.